Jeff Baldwin
January 9, 2002

Nancy
Barton
Feb 2002

HOOSIER FARMBOY
IN LINCOLN'S ARMY

HOOSIER FARMBOY IN LINCOLN'S ARMY

The Civil War Letters of
Pvt. John R. McClure
of the 14th Indiana Regiment

Compiled and Edited by
NANCY NIBLACK BAXTER

GUILD PRESS OF INDIANA, INC.

GUILD PRESS OF INDIANA, INC.
435 Gradle Drive
Carmel, Indiana 46032
317-848-6421
www.guildpress.com

ISBN 0-9617367-2-0

Printed and bound in the United States of America

Illustrated by Richard Day

Table of Contents

Preface to this real-life story by the owner of the Civil War letters

John R. McClure was my maternal grandfather. He was born five miles from Vincennes, Indiana, on a farm given to his great-grandfather Daniel McClure as a bonus for service in the Revolutionary War. I went to live with my grandfather when I was three years old, upon the death of my mother, and heard many times of his exploits as a private in the Fourteenth Indiana Volunteers in the Civil War.

The letters in this collection were found in a secret compartment of an old bureau in the farmhouse on the old place, which I now own. They were written to his sister Mary and "the girl he left behind," Frances Anne Purcell, whom he married in 1866.

John R. died in 1923 and is buried in the churchyard of the first Protestant church in Indiana, the Upper Indiana Presbyterian Church, which was founded by his great-grandfather Daniel and other Scotch-Irish pioneers in 1806.

--Judge John L. Niblack, Former Circuit Court Judge, Marion County, Indianapolis.

Introduction

In the spring of 1861, a steady stream of young men made their way through the valleys of the Wabash River in Indiana on horseback or rode railway cars northward. On April 12, Ft. Sumter had been fired on. These were some of the first volunteers of the Civil War hurrying to join Lincoln's army.

Among them was eighteen-year-old John R. McClure of Knox County, Indiana. This is his story as told in letters from the battlefields to his family and friends back home. He was a private in the Fourteenth Regiment of the famous Gibraltar Brigade of the Army of the Potomac—the first Indiana regiment to be organized for three-years duty.

John McClure grew up on a farm in southern Indiana in the years 1843-1860. His parents had died when he was very young, and his aunt and uncle, who lived next door to the family farm, reared him.

John did not have much schooling. He was expelled in the fifth grade for mischief. He turned a hog loose in the school house, and it wrecked quite a few desks before it was caught. After that, John spent his time helping his Uncle Archie plant and harvest wheat and corn.

The Civil War came to America when John was only eighteen. He had known that his neighborhood and state were alarmed at arguments over slavery in the South before 1860. New states were coming into the Union, and the South wanted them to be slave states while the North wanted the new states to be free. John did not particularly approve of slavery, and he was very angry when he heard the South had "seceded." Eleven states left the Union to form the Confederate States of America, so they could have slaves and decide their own future.

Finally, on April 12, after Abraham Lincoln was inaugurated as President, Southerners took over a federal fort, (Sumter in North Carolina) by firing massive cannons in bombardment.

War broke out between the North and the South and John and his cousin Henderson Simpson left right away to join the Northern Army. They did not go to free the slaves at that point, but to keep the United States one nation.

John McClure's spelling and grammar are rough and often incorrect. We have left them as they were in the original letters.

Nancy N. Baxter
Cathedral High School
Indianapolis

Civil War Events in *Hoosier Farmboy in Lincoln's Army.*

Southern States secede from Union	December, 1860-February, 1861
Lincoln is Inaugurated	March 4, 1861
Fort Sumter is bombarded	April 12-13, 1861
West Virginia Campaign	July-Nov., 1861
First Bull Run (Manassas)	July 21, 1861
Shenandoah Valley Battles	Summer, 1862
Seven Days Battles near Richmond	June 25 - July 1, 1862
Second Bull Run (Second Manassas)	Aug. 29-30, 1862
Battle of Antietam	Sept. 17, 1862
Emancipation Proclamation issued	Sept. 23, 1862
Battle of Fredericksburg	Dec. 13, 1862
Battle of Chancelorsville	May 2 - 4, 1863
Vicksburg on the Mississippi falls, West is lost by the South	July 4, 1863

Gettysburg	July 1,2,3, 1863
New York Draft Riots	July, Aug., 1863
Battle of Wilderness	May 5,6, 1864
Battles: Spotsylvania, Cold Harbor	May, June, 1864
Sherman's March	Nov. - Dec. 1864
Appomattox: General Lee surrenders to General Grant	April 9, 1865

Magazines like *Leslie's* or *Harper's* had illustrations showing sad partings when soldiers left their homes. Many sentimental songs were written during the war. This verse from a popular ballad shows the sadness families felt at the death of a loved one in the war.

> We shall meet, but we shall miss him
> There will be a vacant chair
> We will linger to caress him
> When we breathe our evening prayer.

> *"The Vacant Chair"*

The Wabash River Valley ...

Home of "The Young Americans,"

John R. McClure, Henderson Simpson and their friends

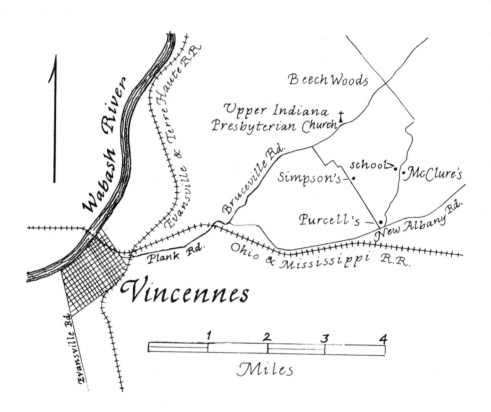

John went into the Fourteenth Indiana Regiment, which was organized to be 1,000 men—ten companies of one-hundred men from several different towns. They met at "rendezvous camp" to learn how to be soldiers, to drill and to shoot muskets and the new rifles they would use. Rendezvous sites were like big summer camps, with lots of joking and game playing to accompany strategy lessons. Some men signed on for only a year but most, like those in the Fourteenth, realized it would take longer and signed the roll for three years.

They boasted they would "get the scalp" of Jeff Davis—Jefferson Davis, the President of the Confederacy. John wrote excited, confident letters to his sisters Mary Jane and Annie and brother Bob.

Camp Vigo
May the 7th '61

Dear Sister

Your letter found me in good health and spirits. I was glad to hear from you, you cannot imagine how much good it does me to get a letter. We are most of us going for three years. The one year fellows started yesterday to Richmond, Ind. There was 27 went out of our company; they will be distributed out amonxt other strange companys. We all go together the way we was. We expect to get home as quick as the one year men!

I got a letter last night that only contained eight pages. SHE said that she was out at your house last Sunday,[1] said you was all well.

---

[1]"She" being Frances Purcell, his future wife.

I got a box the other day from home that had some nice cake and pie etc. It was real nice. We are going to be sworn in today or tomorrow and then some of us will come home. The colonel said all of the three year men could come home but we cannot all come at once; we can stay three or four days. Tell Mart Johnson if he wants to go along with us fellows now is his chance. If he will come up here he can have a chance to join our company. I expect we will start for virginna in a week or so. I am going after Jef Davises scalp! Sis it is to hot for me to write any more at present. Give my best respects to all the folks. Write soon,

Yours Truely

Mr. John R. McClure

Tell Miss Ann I think she might write me a letter. You must not make so many excuses in your letters.

John thought that after being trained, the regiment would go to Virginia to help defend Washington, D.C., but instead they went to Indianapolis, the capitol city, to await orders. They did get guns, some of the Enfield rifles which fired little cone bullets known as Minié balls. But there wasn't much to do except go to a July 4th picnic and be lazy while they waited to go fight Rebels.

Indianapolis
Camp Kimble, June 30th 61

Dear Sister
    It is Sunday and I have not much to do and consequently I am going to write a few letters and thought I would write you a few lines to let you know that I am well and hope you are enjoying the

same blessing. We have got our tents, six sleeps in one tent. The regiment looks somewhat like a little town. There is about 5,000 souldiers encamped around Indianapolis. The thirteenth regiment will leave for for Virginia this eavening, I expect, and tomorow the fifteenth is expected to leave.

Our Regiment (14 reg) will leave soon. I wish we could get off where we would have something to do. I dont like to be laying around. We get so lazy some of the boys cant hardly walk. I expect you folks have fine times since all the bad boys left! Do you have any picnics? Where are you going the 4th? I expect you folks have fine times. I wish I could be down there on the 4th. The citizens of this city are talking about getting up a celebration. I expect we will be invited. I supose Mart Johnson is not going for the war, tell him he had better go. He will see the elephant. The old post guards got a half-grown gosling with them, they got it down at Terehaute.

The Fourteenth Regiment adopted a small goose in rendezous camp.

They say they are going to take it with them through the wars. We are not going to the wars with the old muskets, we are going to get good guns enfield rifles I guess. Have you saw bill Carnan since he come home, he got an honorable discharge. I guess he was very glad to get home. I guess we will get a discharge when ever the war is over. What does unkle Archy have to say on the war subject any how? I expect you have plenty of cherries and mulberries down at your house. I have not tasted any thing of the kind since in camp. I believe I ate one cherry. I must come to close, no more at present.

Yours Truely
Mr. J. R. McClure

Miss Annie

I was very glad to hear from you. How is all the folks at your house any how. If you are a good cook I would be very much obliged to you if you would send me and bud up a nice pie or to in a little box, that is if it is not too much trouble. no more at pressent.

Yours Truely
John R. Mc.

The war heated up in the East, as Rebels tried to capture important cities, roads, or railroad centers in the North. Finally on the move to Lincoln's Army, John McClure and his Northern regiment left on the railroad "cars," crossing the Ohio River. They went into western Virgina, which the North was trying to take away from the South. They were put on the top of Cheat Mountain, a cold and rainy spot, not too far from Robert E. Lee and the Southern army. Henderson "Bud" Simpson wrote the first part of the letter, which is full of jokes about a friend of John's and Bud's, Mart Johnson, who stayed home. They have nicknamed their group of friends at home the Young Americans.

to Miss Mary Jane McClure

Cheat Mountain Summit
18th Aug(1861)

Dear Cousin

I have delayed writing to you so long that I am almost ashamed to commence. But better late than never, besides I want to hear from you, how all the "Young Americans" are getting along. I have not heard from one of them (excepting you) since I left home last time. I hear that you have had several partys lately. How I would like to see you all together again. I hope I shall have the pleasure of meeting you all again. But I am afraid that the time is far distant. I suppose the "Young Americans" will call themselves ladies and jentlemen, by the time we get back. I suppose "Mart" is splurging about as usual, talking of going to war and all that kind of thing; but "Mother" wont let him. Tell him that without he is very keen for the war, he had better let soldiering alone. For he could not go to see the Girls nor eat apples and peaches or anything else good to eat or drink. This would go too hard with the poor boy. I have not spoken to or seen a girl for six weeks. They are a "skase" article out here. But although we are deprived of conveniences and pleasures, yet the men are in fine spirits and enjoy good health. In fact I do not believe that there are more than three of four sick (they are not dangerous) in the whole Regiment. We have not lost a man by sickness since the Regiment was mustered into service. But, one of the sargents in Capt Woods company was killed as he was going around trying our guards after nightfall to see if they would shoot. They told him to halt but as he would not, they shot him thinking he was a Rebel. Another man of Capt Woods company (Wm. Wilkison) was killed while out scouting besides two or three cavalry men from a company attached to our Regiment. This is all we have lost as yet. But we have amply revenged their loss. One of men (Summer field from Evansville)

7

while out on a scout day before yesterday killed one of the scamps and severely wounded another. Yesterday evening about seventy five of our men went out. They came upon a party of the Rebels early this morning. They pursued them killing nine of them and wounding several other. Our men while pursuing them ran almost into their camp before they knew it but our men retreated without losing a man. Our men all come in this evening. They brought in three splendid horses and nine guns which they took from the F.F.V.'s.[2] They report that this enemy is encamped on Green Brier river twelve miles from here. There are about two thousand of them. Our men when they pursued the squad of cowards killed two of the rebels after they had got into their camp in sight of their whole force. They fired at our men and although some of the balls whistled close enough to our "boys" heads to make them dodge yet none of them were hurt and all are now safe in camp.

[2]First Families of Virginia—the wealthy Southerners.

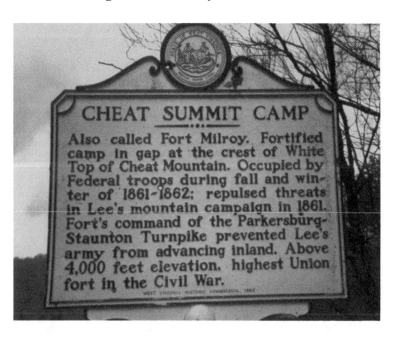

Cheat Mountain camp is marked in West Virginia with an historic marker.

It would make you laugh to see our camp. It has been raining so much (it has been raining all morning) that we had to pave our streets with stone to keep out of the mud. Ten of us have built a log house to cook in, we have a good chimbly which draws well. Our house is built of spruce fir logs and covered with spruce bark. It is a very good covering and keeps every thing dry. It seems more like home on a rainy day. We sit by a bright fire in a dry house (Shantys we call them) and cook our meals. How I would enjoy a dinner at home now for I have not set down at a table to eat for six weeks. But nevertheless we have plenty to eat and we know how to cook it.

(The above portion of this letter was not signed, but evidently was written by Henderson "Bud" Simpson)

Dear Sis,
    While Mr. Simpson is writing I thought I would write a little to. I am well at pressent and have been ever since I left home. This is an awful country out here, nothing but rocks and big hills, for all that we are doing very well. I suppose you heard of the battle out there.
    Bully old battle,[3] next morning the ground was thick with dead secesionists. The best of it was before the battle the rascals dug two big long graves to bury union men in but instead of the union men being buried in it the holes was filled with their own men. There is no news out here, we cannot hear much out in these mountains. The sesessionists have all left; if they see a union man they run like a turkey. If we stay here I dont think we will get much fighting to do. If Gen Scotts boys all makes the old Secesh get like we have since we have been here it will not take long to clean them

[3] Really a skirmish(small battle or exchange of gunfire) with part of Lee's army.

out. Tell no more at pressent. Give my best respects to all. Write soon.

    If you will send me some old newspapers it will please me very much.

Yours Truely

John R. McClure

The Fourteenth Regiment were acting as scouts among the "Secessionists" (the Southerners who had seceded from the United States). Scouts went out to see where the enemy were located and their troop numbers. Often they met "Secesh" when they didn't want to. John has quit joking in his letters now. He knows the war is serious—some men have been shot on scout duty and one friend had to have his hand amputated following a gunshot accident.

Cheat Mount Pass
August 23 rd 1861

Sister Mary

    I take pleasure in sitting down to answer your welcome letter of which I received a few days since. I am all right at pressent the only thing that bothers me we have most too much rain and it is rather cold up here too. I suppose you folks are having fine times now days, eating fruit, watermelons etc. I wish I were there about a week to help you for all we are living very high out here on

10

crackers, bacon etc. I received a letter from Tont & Mag the other day it is the first one that I have had from home since I have been in Virginia. It stated that you beech woods folks have had fine times lately going to parties etc. We are doing big works here on the mountain cutting down trees, building batteries killing a Secesh evry once in a while, but they get one of us evry once in a while to. I supose you heard about Bill Wilkerson getting shot by the rebles while out skouting, there was a cavalryman wounded and annother one killed at the same time. One of the boys in the evansville company shot his hand off accidently while putting the bayonet on his gun. His hand had to be taken off. Our mess has built a hut. It goes very well when it is rainy cold day, and that is all the time you might say. The other night the field officers was afraid of attack, had the 17 reg to come up on the hill in the night. The next morning I awoke up, put on my shoes, steped out, and who do you think I saw stepping around with a sword hanging to his side? It was Dick Hargrave. I guess you know him, he inquired all about you and Ann Mag McCord, etc how you folks in the beech woods were getting along. Dick is 1st Lieutenant in one of the companies in the 17th regiment—he looks as savage as a meat axe. Yesterday eavening we took three prisoners one horseman, one man and a team and waggon and a little boy. They come inside of our pickets before they knew it I supose. The furthest squad of pickets saw them and hid at the side of the road let them pass and then closed in on the dads. The rest of the company has to go to night on picket guard about 3 miles over on the hill towards the secesh camp. I dont have to go, I am a wood chopper, there is 10 choppers in the company & I am one of them.

I believe I will come to a close. Just tell the folks I will be at home in 3 years maby.

Yours Truely

John R. McClure

John McClure and the rest of the Fourteenth fought their first real battle on September 12, 1861—the Battle of Cheat Mountain. Robert E. Lee attempted to find and fight the Northern Army but was pushed back. The Fourteenth continued to cut the forest down to make defensive stockade walls. Lack of uniforms was becoming a problem in the cold mountain climate, and some soldiers had badly torn pants.

Cheat Mount Pass, VA.
Sept 18, 1861

Sister Mary

We have had right stressing times here for the last few days. I believe evry thing has cooled down now. The Secesh tried to run us out of our nests but I guess they have gave it up as a bad job, we killed about 100 of them. It did not take but 2 or three companies to run them. Capt Coons was out skouting with part of his companies; I was along with him, we had a prety sharp skirmish (See Vincennes Gazette. Will describe the proceedings) The Secesh balls whistled close to my skull I tell you but not one totched it. Jo Cambell had a ball to go through his hat. September 21st—I comenced this letter day before yesterday but did not get to finish it so I will commence again. I would have writen to you sooner but the secesh has been tolarble thick about here and the mail could not go through very handy but it has been going through for the last few days. It is not raining now but it rained last night like blazes, was coldest kind. The bloody 14th has not got clothes yet. The colonel sent word to where ever the clothes was to come from and told them his regiment could not stay on the hill much longer if we did not get them. I got a letter from Bob yesterday. I will answer it soon. You aught to have been here to see Bud put on style with his new pants that he got from home, evry body saying helow Simpson where did you get so much pants. My old pants holds out very well. I think they will last a good while yet. If we stay here much longer we will have a big farm cleared for Old Mr. White. We are cutting the timber down all around, he is a brother to the White that use to live on our place. I supose you have fine times now; I think I could stow a few of them away. There is not much prospect of a fight with the secesh now without we go after them. I dont think we will get the chance to go for them for awhile, any way it is about supper time and I must eat you know. No more at present. Write soon

Yours truly

John R. McClure

Give my respects to all.

Life in camp centered around the campfire.

Cheat Mountain Sumit, Va
October 2 ond, 1861

Sister Mary,

I take pleasure in seating myself in my tent to answer your letter of which I received this morning. Henderson is well, he thinks it is curious that he has received no letters for some time. He got the basket of things which his mother sent him. I got the paper and envelops which you sent me and also a letter from Ann. There has been nothing strange turned up on the hill for the last few days only we have got our long tailed blue overcoats and pants, we will get our pay and the rest of our clothes soon I guess. I wrote a letter to Abe Snapp this morning, wrote one to Bob day before yesturday. I suppose you have heard of the great attact which the Secesh made not long since. They played smash generaly. We made them get up and how prety fast. Me and about 60 other boys were out skouting with Capt Coons the same day they attacted Our camp. We got into a nest of about 2000. We killed several of them then concluded we had better get out of there. They did not kill one of us.

I wrote you a letter about a week ago but thought I would write you a short letter so that I would not get behind the time. There is only 9000 of us on the hill now. I think the secesh will have a sweet time before long. You said in your letter that you had a great deal of work to do caning peaches and so forth. I wish I had some of your caned fruit here. There is some talk of us leaving this hill for winter quarters, of course there will be one or two regiments left here but I dont guess it will be our regiment. They say that there may be such a thing as us to be placed down on the Ohio River, I only hope we may. We have a preacher in our regiment. I have not much to write this morning and had better come to a close promising to write a longer letter the next time no more at pressent.

Yours Truely

John R. McClure

Soon, however, the Fourteenth was ordered off the mountain. The army was being shifted around. Actually, the North wasn't doing very well. The army further east had lost the battle of Bull Run in the summer and was having other problems, and the generals were moving troops around trying to make their effort stronger.

John is mad at the "sweet little boys who won't come join the army" like he did.

Camp at Hutonville, VA
Nov 11th

Dear Sister

It is with pleasure that I take my pensil in hand to answer your most welcome letter which I received not long since. I am well at pressent and hope you and the folks are enjoying the same. There is not much new or any thing else in camp now days. All got quiet since we came off the mountain but we are beginning to want to get away from here as bad as we did off the mountain. Us boys would like to get into Kentucky where humane beings lives. Good deal of game out there too.

What you folks call Secesh. But us Virginians calls them Secesh. They are not quite so many as they use to be; one thing certain they cant stay in these mountains long, not many of them at least, because the roads are so bad they cannot get provission. And it is the same way with us. That is one thing that makes me think we will get out of here before long. The roads are very bad but I think the Secesh has a harder time halling their provision over the Allegany than we do. The word was in evry boddies mouth last saturday that we would go to building winter quarters today but today has come and we are not building winter quarters and I am very glad of it, for I do not want to stay out here this winter. I think that we aught to go some place and get some more men. We cannot muster more than 600 men that is able for duty in the regiment, but what is left of us are bully boys.

How are things getting along about home by this time? Is evry thing all right—is the many sweet little men about there? Tell them to be good little boys and take good care of the girls.

How is Andy Purcell getting along up at Johns? Does he pitch in as strong as he use to? I tell you he is one of the sweet little boys. Sis I will have to come to a close there nothing of importance to write about. Write soon

Yours Truely

John R. McClure

my respect to all the folks

John and his fellow soldiers were being shifted into first one then another town between mountain ranges of the Shenandoah Valley in Virginia. John wrote to his sister and to his girlfriend, Fanny Purcell, telling of life in town and in camp. He is also asking questions about their friends in the old Beech Woods neighborhood at home, and his cousin Tom McClure off in the army somewhere else.

Camp at Phillippi Va
December the 9th, 1861

Sister Mary

I take my pen in hand this morning to write you. I am well at present and hope you are enjoying the same. This is a right nice little place we are staying in now, they say we will stay here all winter. I would not care much if we would. I received a letter from you day before yesterday, was very glad to hear from you. There is not very many folks lives in this city but they are very nice folks what there is of them. I am boarding at a house now and intend to board there for about a week until our cooking utensils come from Huttonville. Our company has taken up quarters at the court house. We have a gay old time now days, nothing to do but lay around no Secesh to bother us. I think you must be behind the times about the news. I heard of Miss Brentlingers wedding about two months ago and I dont know whether I aught to have been there to helped her kill bats or not. I think most likely I aught not have been there. And so Fanny thinks I aught to write to her. ha. Well tell her when ever I feel like writing I will call around. People must think that I have got nothing to do but write. In the first place out here is one of the meanest places to write letters ever was. You can imagine how you could write in a big room where there is about 100 men cutting up all kinds of monkey shines. Tell Anna I will write her a letter before long but I will send her this little book for Christmass gift. This little book is made out of laural root it grows on Cheat Mountain. Sis, I have nothing to send you just now I have no more to write at pressent. Write soon.

Yours Truely

John R. McClure

The flag of the Fourteenth Indiana Regiment as it was re-created by Civil War re-enactors from California.

When John writes to his girlfriend, Frances (or Fanny), his style is different from the way he writes to his family. His letter to Fanny has few spelling errors and lots of big words. Probably he was trying to impress her, and perhaps his cousin Bud helped him with the letter.

Camp at North Fork Bridge,M.D.
Jan 22 nd 1862

Friend Fanny

Yours of the 16th is at hand and I have seated myself down to answer your most welcome letter. You cannot imagine how much good it does a soldier boy like myself to get a letter from old friends. It has been raining here for the last three or four days and you can imagine what good times we are having in our little white houses. We are camped on the Balt and Ohio Railroad six miles east of Cumberland. From the way you write I think the old Americans have been playing particular thunder in that part of the country in which you live such as getting married etc. Dan Smith I supose is satisfied because he has got one of the star spangled banners of the beech woods. Well the captain is going to have an inspection of arms and therefore I will have to lay my pencil down and go. Well my old musket has got some rust on it but it passed and therefore consequently I brought it back and laid it up in the dry to stay there for awhile, not verry long I guess, for I expect that we will go for some secesh before long. We generally, when we start out on such an expedition as that, we start out about twelve o clock at night in order that we may reach our friends camp about day light just in time to take breakfast with them. I got a letter from Tom McClure the other day. He seems to think they are having verry hard times, well I expect they have. I expect Tom thinks that Jordon is a hard road to travel. I would not be very much suprised if there was some other boys in the same fix. Has Deck got that little rifle yet, if he has tell him to take good care of it and when I come home I will come over and show him how to kill squirrels. I told Simpson that you said that you had not got a letter from him for a long time. He says that he is strapped and got no paper but will write as soon as he gets some paper. I think he takes up most of his time writing to Miss Lizzie Kelso[4] I took notice that he got a letter the other day from her that contained about eight pages and I guess he sent her about the same back. You must not tell her that I told you.

Fanny what has become of Andy. Tell him that I would like to hear from him, I believe I have no more to write at pressent and consequently taking every thing into consideration I think I had better come too a close hoping to hear from you soon.

Your sincere friend

John R. McClure

Remember thy creator in
the days of thy youth

Shakespear

Give my best respects to your mother and father also Eliza and Deckar. Bud Simpson told me to tell you that he had not forgotten you.

[4]Whom "Bud" Simpson later married. Decker ("Deck") and Eliza were Fanny Purcell's brother and sister.

Bud Simpson wrote to his cousin thanking her for many "care packages" she sent. Canning of fruits had begun less than ten years before, but was very popular in the United States.

Letter of J. H. Simpson to M. J. McClure, dated February 1, 1862.

Camp at North Branch Bridge, Md.
Feb 1rst

Dear Cousin,

I received your letter last night and real glad I was to hear from you—and this morning having nothing particular to do I thought I would answer your letter. And now if you'll "jist wait till I take a chaw terbacker" I'll stick my feet up against the jam in the "big room" and tell you yarns till dinner-time.

We have had some gloomy wintery weather since we camped here; but then it is no more that what we expect at this season. Waked up this morning and found the ground covered with snow to the depth of six inches—But as far as snow is concerned—I don't believe that we have been out of sight of snow since the first of Nov. for it rarely disappears from the mountain summits during the winter. This certainly must have been a very mild winter or else I can stand cold better than I used to for as yet I havent suffered the least bit from cold; and from now on (with warm clothing you sent me) I bid defiance to old winters coldest blast.

You must have thought we were suffering out from the amount of clothing you sent us—Although I wasn't suffering any yet I was glad to get the many little comforts you sent me—But the white blanket and pants were more than I needed at the present time and having as much as I could conveniently carry without them I thought I would send them home till I wanted them. I think I have enough now to last me til we're discharged. You ought to have seen us pitch into the peaches and black-berries—As I helped each of the mess to some they would remark "that puts me in mind of Indiany" —"bully for old Indiany" and other like remarks were continually going around. I found a bundle of long round things in the box couldn't imagine what they were—but when I unrolled them I had to sit down and take a real good look. Who would have thought of getting white pudding out here—real Hosier pudding. Better believe I wasn't long pitching into it—I put me in mind of the many times I have stood up before the cup-board in the kitchen munching white pudding—Hope it wont be long before I stand there again. We thought them Heath cling peaches the best peaches we ever ate.

As for mitten and gloves I have got five or six pair of them. John got two or three pair from some of the girls in the upper neighborhood. Guess I know who they come from. You asked me about my boots. Well I couldn't get them on at first but I got one of my mess to wear them awhile after that I could get them on tolerably easy most too small though. Who made the jean pants? They're most too small but they'll do first rate. Tell Ma to keep the other pants till I want them. Tell Ma to take good care of those laurel pipes, they come from Cheat mountain. One of them was made by a messmate of mine who was taken prisoner while on the "summit". The old hat has become dear to me from the adventures and scouts we have had to-gether.

The crackers I present to you all as specimen of the bread we have been living on for seven months.

Write soon

to M. J. McClure   Your cousin

                                H. Simpson

P.S. Tell Ma that I receive all her letters but sometimes I get two or three together so she only gets one from me for two or three she writes.

Tell Ma to send me plenty of envelops and stamps for I ought to answer several letters which I cannot for want of stamps and I will send the money for them when we get paid.

Listen for a big fight soon.

I have got several letters here two days after they were mailed.

Accouterments

haversack

cup

eating utensils

coffee beans

hardtack

pipe, tobacco & matches

picture of sweetheart

soap & towel

razor

knife

Jew's harp

money

pen

sewing kit

John McClure, Cousin Bud and the rest didn't have to wait long to fight again. In the spring of '62, General Stonewall Jackson was fighting Northern troops in what is known as the Valley Campaign. General Jackson wanted to stop Union Army troops from going to help fight at Richmond. He went around fighting and confusing different parts of the Northern Army in the Shenandoah Valley so it couldn't go to join General George McClellan's army at Richmond. The Fourteenth met Stonewall's troops at the Battle of Winchester Heights (Kernstown) in late March.

Strausburg, Va. March 28th [1862]

Dear Sister

I once more have the pleasure of seating my self to answer your most welcome letter which I received not long since. I expect you folks has been some what uneasy since the battle we had at Winchester but I can assure you that I am all right yet, there was not a bullet grazed my hide. Henderson got a slight wound in the arm. It will not be long before he will be well. It is of no use for me to tell you any thing about the fight because you can read it in the papers only I can tell you that the 14th done her best. The 13th Ind fought by the side of us all yelling like Indians, there was only four hurt in our company. John Conly got his left fore finger shot off. Mike Mulville slightly wounded in the leg. Tom Balley just tipped the side of his head, it knocked him down but he jumped up and after the secesh again. I dont know whether this letter will get to you or not. They have been talking about not letting letters home for 30 days. Henderson did not get to shoot but three shoots.

I will have to come to a close it is about bed time and I will write again soon

Yours truly

John R. McClure

John set his paycheck ($13 per month) home to sister Mary Jane. She must have complained that not all of it was arriving and accused him of gambling. The following letter tells of hardships and high prices the army was living through. There was no time or money for gambling! Many people at home didn't seem to understand how hard the war was.

Camp near Monassas Junction
June 26th, 1862

Dear Sister

I received your letter yesterday. I was very glad to hear from you. I have not had a chance to write many letters home. We have marched about 400 miles since the 12th of May and you may know how I feel by this time. I stood the march verry well. I am well at pressent. Well now for the question, well sister Mary I think that is a verry foolish question that you want me to answer. Another thing I think I know a little more about these things than you do because you never was a souldier, you dont know how things work out here. I suppose that you are not aware that when we get on a long march and the roads are bad we sometimes are fed on half rations and the verry poorest at that. I have been, while on some marches, I would not see a bite of meat for two or three days. Nothing but sheet iron crackers and coffy with no sugar in it and scarce at that. Well if you have money you can get a meals victuals for from twenty five cts to fifty, any thing you buy you will have to pay like thunder for it. I dont think that I have spent my money foolishly. If you get a pair of boots out here I have to pay $7.00 for them, but I guess that I will go to wearing old government shoes and keep my feet wet half the time. Just suspose to send my little old $13.00 dollars a month home. And another thing the way you write it seems as though you dont put verry much confidence in me, you are afraid I will go to gambling. I thought that you knowed that I had more sense than to gamble my money away. You never knowed of me gambling while at home or out here either. You must reckollect that you folks are seeing good times to what us fellows do out here.

I have no more to write at present.

Write soon to your Brother

John R. McClure

John, Bud and the rest of the Fourteenth were ordered to leave the Shenandoah Valley and join the rest of the Yankee army near the Southern capitol of Richmond. The Seven Days Battles were being fought June 25- July 1 1862 so the North could take Richmond, the Southern capital.

The attempt failed, and the Fourteenth arrived at the end of the battles, just in time to help the Northern Army retreat. General McClellan pulled the Yankees back to the James River to await travelling back to Washington, DC. John watched "pickets," soldiers put out before the main troops to watch for trouble. Northern and Southern pickets were so close they talked to each other and exchanged tobacco and newspapers. Mart Johnson has finally come to join the Fourteenth.

Camp on James River

July 13th, 1862

Dear Sister

I received your letter this morning. It came yesturday but I was on guard all night and did not get it until this morning. I am in good health at pressent. Simpson and Mart is here all right. You stated in your letter that you expected that we were fighting while you were writing the letter. I think that you was mistaken you must not think that we fight all the time. We had a little skirmish the next day after we landed here. There was no one killed in our regt only six wounded none in Comp G. Ever thing is quiet along the whole line. The Secesh has fallen back I dont know how far though. When we first came here our pickets and the secesh pickets were not more than 150 yds apart. Sometimes our boys and the secesh would lay down their guns and meet half way and talk for an hour perhaps. I nevver tried the experiment. There has been some heavy old fighting just before we came here we are now about 25 miles from Richmond I suppose you have heard of McClellen falling back to this posision. we have a splendid posishon. Here is our posish

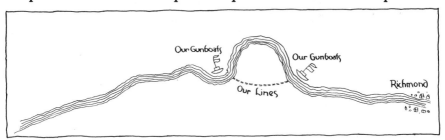

Mart Johnson is getting along as well as could be expected. He dont like hard crackers and fat meat verry well. I have not much to write about today as Simpson wants to write I will leave space for him. No more at pressent. Write soon.

Your Brother

John R. McClure

Direct to care
  Capt Coons
  Co G 14th Ind Vol
Harrisons Landing, Kimballs Brigade
Smiths Division Franklin Corps
Via Fortress Monroe, Va.

Sunday morning

Cousin Mary

Tell Ma to send me the New York Ledger and the Mercury every week—I will send the money as soon as I am paid.

Cant get a paper here of any kind for less that from ten to twenty five cents. Have nothing to read at all. I suppose John had told you all the news. You say that you havent yet received Marts carpet [bag.] We expressed it from Indianapolis on 25th of June directed to his Mother. I sent a picture of mine in it. Havent seen the original of that picture yet, have you? John accidently saw it. He wants to know who it is. Write soon—if you consider this worth answering.

Bud

General McClellan sadly realized he could not take the Rebel Capital of Richmond. It was too well defended by Robert E. Lee and the other Generals and too many men had died trying to advance on the city. McClellan decided to take the Yankees back North and John prepared to go with his Regiment by boat.

U.S. and Confederate sentries met between the lines on the James River.

Harrisons Landing— Va.
August 14 th 1862

Dear Sister

I received your letter the other day was verry glad to hear from you. It found me in good health and I hope when these few lines reaches you they will find you enjoying the same. Mart is getting along very well. Ever thing has been quiet on the James for some time. I think we will make a move from here before long. I dont know where all of our knapsacks have been shipped on the boats and I suppose we will follow soon. I have not much to write this morning. Capt Coons is Comander of the regt. I met with a little bad luck yesterday. I lost my pocket book with about $15 in it and besides a $20 note I had on one of our boys but it is good any how. I sent $30 home to Unkle bob I dont know whether he has got it or not but I supose he has by his time.
No more at pressent.
Your Brother

Jno. R. McClure

The Fourteenth Regiment returned by boat in August 1862 to the area around Washington D.C. and participated in the end of the Second Battle of Bull Run or Second Manassas. Then, John McClure grew ill, and was sent to the hospital. While he was sick, the Fourteenth Regiment fought the great battle of Antietam, called the "Greatest day of bloodshed on the American continent," Sept. 17,1862. The Fourteenth fought so well at "Bloody Lane," losing half of its men killed or wounded, that Commanding General William French named the regiment and two others who fought with it "The Gibraltar Brigade."

Washington Co, M.D.

Sept 24th 1862

Dear Sister

I received your most welcome letter some days ago I was very glad to hear from you. We had a verry hot time out here last Wednesday, there was one of the hardest fought battles as ever was known on the American Continent. As luck would have it I was not in the fight I was left at Rockville near Washington sick but I am getting stout now. I am not with the regt now. I am staying at the Hospital near the battle field with our Wounded boys. Our company had two men killed and eleven wounded, Capt Coons was Wounded. Thomas Thompson was shot with a musket ball above the ankle one bone in his leg is broken. The other boys are not badly wounded; you are not acquainted with them. John J. Tanderman was killed, also R. N. Kelso, they were both killed dead on the field. To take it all together the Secesh got badly whipped. Our regt went into the fight 400 strong and come out with 210 sound men, that was killing and wounding nearly half. I have not more to write at pressent.

Give my best respects to all the folks and tell them I am all right. Mart and Bud Simpson was not in the fight.

Write soon to your Brother

John R. McClure

The two armies-the North and South–stopped fighting for a while and went into camp near each other. John McClure was still ill, and stayed with the wagons while the rest of the soldiers fought the Battle of Fredericksburg, Dec. 13, 1862. General Burnside, who had replaced General McClellan, tried to break through Robert E. Lee's lines on the banks of the Rapidan and Rappahannock rivers. The Northeners couldn't

get "on to Richmond" as long as Lee's army blocked the way. Lee was
on the top of a hill called Marye's Heights. The Yankees down below
were ordered to "storm the hill" running across open fields to take it.
The attack didn't work; General Burnside had a poor plan, and the
Yankees got shot down by soldiers and cannons on the hill. Nine
thousand Northerners were killed. John was back across the river,
where new reserve troops waited to cross, fight and be shot. Stretcher
carriers brought in the wounded and surgeons amputated arms and
legs on the table right before the eyes of troops waiting to go into aciton.
The Battle of Fredericksburg was an awful moment in a terrible war.

Camp near Fredericksburg
Dec 19th 1862

Dear Sister

It is with pleasure that I seat my self down this morning to write
you a few lines to let you know that I am still alive. I have been
under the weather for some time but I am getting better now. We
had a big fight over here, Fredericksburg, got whipped like thunder. I was not able to be in the fight. Jno McClure[5] could not be
found on the battle field I guess he is killed or taken prisoner but
I am afraid he is dead. He is the only one missing in our company.
Sis I dont know what you think about the war but I will tell you
what I think and that is the north will nevver whip the south as long
as there is a man left in the south. They fight like wild devles. Ever
man seems determined to loose the last drop of blood before they
give up but there is no use of you and I talking about the war
because we cant end it, but I dont care how soon it is stopped.
Christmas will soon be here I would like to be at [home.] I think
I would get a pack of [fire] crackers and go down to unkle Arches
and pop them but in stead of that I am out here in Va eating hard
crackers and bacon but I hope the time will soon come when I can
eat hot buiskets to. Tell Henderson that Sol Gundersun is Orderly.

Union soldiers had to go across a river, down along a narrow road and across a field as they tried unsuccessfully to storm Marye's Heights in the Battle of Fredericksburg, December 1862.

I would like to hear from him I wrote a letter to him not long ago.

I have no news to write to you. I will stop writing for the pressent hoping to hear from you soon. I ever remain your affectionate brother.

Jno. R. McClure

Give my best respects to all the folks tell them to write. I have not received a letter from any one for a long time.

[5] A distant relative of John R's. At the time the Fourteenth was mustered in, "Our John" added "R" as his middle initial to avoid confusion with the several other John McClures in the regiment.

Colonel Nathan Kimball of John's regiment was made a Northern brigadier general following the battle of Winchester Heights.

Bud Simpson and the boys' friend Mart Johnson were discharged because of wounds. John McClure and the rest of the Northern Army were discouraged—in the early months of 1863 the South seemed impossible to beat and the war dragged on while more and more men were wounded and died.

Lincoln had issued the Emancipation Proclamation freeing the slaves, but John didn't care. He was so angry at the war that he began to blame the slaves—they were the cause of it all weren't they? It is a mistake to believe that only Southerners in that time believed Negroes were inferior. Many men in the Union Army, as well as their folks back home, were openly racist from time to time. This letter is full of anger and prejudice, but since John later in his life had black friends and lived in friendship with several Afro-Americans, we can only believe he didn't mean it all. Still, John was wrong—the slave was not to blame for the war and racial prejudice is never right. What John McClure was really angry at was the Civil War.

Camp near Falmoth
Jan 2nd, 1863

Dear Sister

I received your most welcome letter the other day. I was very glad to hear from you. I am tolerable well at present. I wrote a letter to you about two weeks ago, I expect you have got it before this.

What kind of Christmas and New Year did you have. I expect you certainly had a better time than I. I had fat pork and crackers for dinner and crackers and fat pork for supper. What appears to be the matter with Henderson, was he discharged on account of his wound or what kind of sickness? What has become of Mart Johnson? I did hear that he got a discharge if he has got it I say bully for him because I think the Union is about played out. I use to think that we were fighting for the union and constitution but we are not. We are fighting to free those colored gentlemen. If I had my way about things I would shoot ever nigger I come across.

I am thinking of old Abe makes his words true you folks will have an awful bad smell amonxt you by the time we get home, get all the niggars on an equality with you. But I dont think old Abe and all the rest of his niggar lovers can free the slaves because the south has a little to say about that. Old Abe has got to whip the south first and that is a thing that he will not do very soon. Well that is enough about the war. How is things in old Indianna by this time. I want you to write to me and post me all about the times at home. There is no use talking about me writing an interesting letter out here for there is nothing to be seen only big headed Officers and big guns.

Tell Miss Ann I think she might stick a few lines in your letter and send to me.

I believe I have no more to write at present. Write as soon as you can to your Brother.

Jno. R. McClure

Give my respects to all.

I heard that Isack Purcell was killed and robbed. Trent Landon saw a tellegraph dispach to that effect anyhow. Is there any thing of it–

"Sis, I was demoralized last winter," John admits in the next letter meaning he was very discouraged and not himself. Now, though, he is joking again and hoping battle won't start up too soon. That was because he was just beginning to feel better after losing a lot of weight, and was weak from stomach flu or dysentery which actually killed more men in the Civil War than did battles.

But battle waits for no man. The roads of Virginia were drying and Joe Hooker, the new Northern general, wanted to take the army south again— fighting Lee's army which was spread out blocking all roads to Richmond. Break through Lee's army lines, destroy the army, go to the Rebel capital city, end the war—that was the idea. The Battle of Chancellorsville , May of 1863, was coming and John couldn't rest a moment longer.

Back home again in Indiana, a new and unpopular draft law was bringing more soldiers to regiments which had lost many men. Unless a young man paid a $300 fee to get a substitute, or unless he got married, he had to go at once.

Falmoth, Va. April 1 st, 63

Dear Sister

It is with pleasure that I seat my self this windy morning to write you a few lines to let you know how I am getting along.

I am in verry good health at pressent and I hope these few lines may find you enjoying the same blessing.

I think that I answered your last letter but probably you did not get it and I thought I would write another one. We are having verry good times out here now but we may have to march soon but I hope not for I never did like to march. I expect the reason that you have not written, you wanted to let all the folks get married in order that you might tell me about it all in one letter but I guess if they have not got three hundred $ they will have to come out any how. I do think that there has been more folks married since I left than was ever heard of before. I never get a letter from any of the girls but what some one is married. Sis I was demoralised last winter in fact I did not think that I would ever be fit for service any more. I just felt like that I did not care for any thing union or no union, of course I will not be able to stand the marching like I have done but in time I think I will be as stout as ever.

Governor Morton was out to see us the other day; he made a short speech to our regt. He told us that the old regt would be filled with conscripts. I think that will be about right. I wont ask them to go through any more than we will. I have no more to write at pressent. Write soon to your Brother

Jno R. McClure

Tell Henderson I would like to hear from him, he owes me a letter.

J.R.

Confederate General Thomas J. "Stonewall" Jackson was named "Stonewall" when he stood like a wall at First Bull Run. He was shot by mistake by his own Rebel soldiers at the Battle of Chancelorsville.

Chancellorsville, fought May 2-4, 1863 was a loss to the North. John and the rest of the Fourteenth and Northern troops were camped in the late afternoon of May 2 awaiting action when Stonewall Jackson's men surprised the Yankees by marching in secret around the flank, or end of the army. In the confusion of fighting and in the retreat that followed, the Northern Army was defeated—or at least was unable to break Lee's lines and had to go back to its camp! "General Hooker lost his nerve," the disgusted Northern soldiers said.

Camp near Falmoth Va
May 10 th - 1863

Dear Sister

It is with pleasure that I seat myself this beautiful morning to let you know that I am all right. I was in the fight never got even a scratch. I will not have time to write much. Colonel Coons is going home and I thought I would send a few lines to let you know that I was well and hearty. Give all the folks my best respects and tell Henderson to write to me.

From your Brother

Jno R. McClure

Write Soon.

In the following letter, John is hearing good reports of a new general, Ulysses S. Grant. Grant was making a name for himself valiantly trying to capture Vicksburg on the Mississippi River. John hopes perhaps Grant could replace the bad commanders in the Army of the Potomac (John's army). The letter mentions the "balloon assention"—a one-man hot air balloon going up to spy on the Rebel camps nearby.

39

Ulysses S. Grant

George Meade

Camp near Falmoth, VA
June 12 th, 63

Dear Sister

I received your letter three days ago it found me well and hearty and I hope these few lines may find you enjoying the same. News is very dry out here not much going on. Our regiment presented General French with a fine swoard the other day, it cost three hundred and twenty five dollars. I tell you it made the old fellow wink. We are under marching orders one half of the time, I dont know how it will be yet, we may have to march soon and we may not. I just now heard the report of four or five cannon. Our balloon made an assention this morning and the rebs are shooting at it from across the rivver. I tell you the old balloon came down again about as quick as she went up. I got a letter from Tom Thompson last night. He says that he can walk without a crutch. I hope he will get entirely well, he seems to talk as though he would like to come out to the army again. I think he had better stay where he is. In your last letter you spoke of Wicks the fellow that was at home on a furlough. You said that you suposed that I was acquainted with him. I should think I aught to be he has been one of my mess mates nearly ever since we come out, he is a good fellow to. I have been listening to hear of the capture of Vicksburg. I hope that Old Grant will put things through. I believe that he is a man that will do it if he can. I will bring my letter to a close hoping to hear from you soon.

From your Brother

John R. McClure

Give my respects to all.
Tell Anna that I have not forgot her yet.

By June, 1863, after Chancellorsville, Robert E. Lee ,the great Confederate general, wished to go on the offensive and break through to winning the war. To cause fear among the people of the North so they would demand peace, and to find food for both men and animals, he entered the rich farmlands of Pennsylvania.

In late June the Northern Army, to be led by General George Meade, marched after Lee through awful heat and pouring rain and ran into Lee almost by chance at a little town called Gettysburg.

165,000 men fought for three terrible days. The first day the South seemed to win, but Generals Richard Ewell and Robert E. Lee let the North get on a hill called Cemetery Hill, and thus get an advantage.

The evening of the second day the Southern troops tried to capture the Northern cannons on top of the hill. It was a decisive moment in the battle and the war.The Fourteenth Regiment—the reliable old Gibraltar Brigade—was called in to rush up and save the cannons and the day for the North. They succeeded and the North still held the hill.

The third day the Fourteenth waited by the edge of Cemetery Hill. In the main part of the battlefield, 15,000 Southern troops under General Pickett charged the Northerners on the hill. This great event was called Pickett's Charge. It failed for the South, and Lee's troops had to retreat out of Pennsylvania.

John McClure's friends in the Fourteenth Indiana were all in the Battle of Gettysburg. John had been left in a little town near the battlefield to watch the wagons.

Dear Sister I seat myself this rainey morning under a waggon to let you know that I am all right yet. We have had some very hard fighting out here at least people says so for my part I was not there. I have not seen the regt since the fight. The morning before the fight Capt Patterson sent me to the waggons to take care of the company things and I am here yet. I dont know where the regiment is. I did hear the particulars about our company. I guess there was only one killed that was Will Dunn from Brucevile.

I cant write much of letter this morning the paper is getting wet now. Write soon to you Brother,

Jno. R. McClure

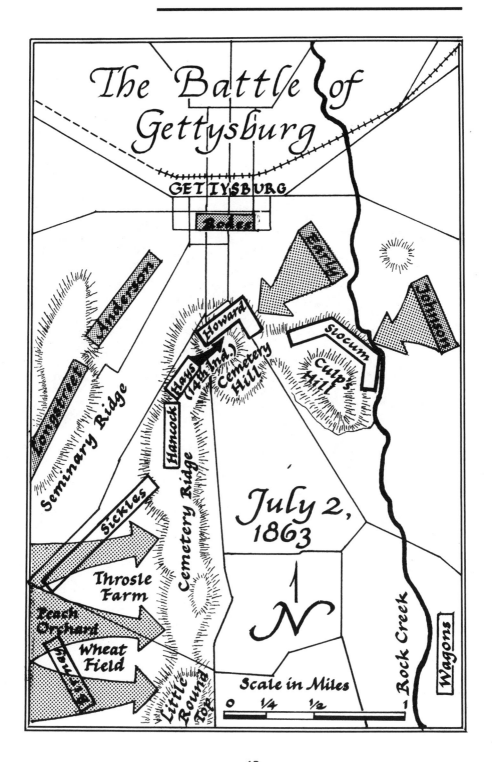

The Battle of Gettysburg

GETTYSBURG

Roder

Ewell

Johnson

Anderson

Pender

Seminary Ridge

Howard

Hays (14th Ind.)

Cemetery Hill

Slocum

Culp's Hill

Hancock

Cemetery Ridge

Sickles

July 2, 1863

N

Throsle Farm

Peach Orchard

Wheat Field

Longstreet

Little Round Top

Scale in Miles

0   ¼   ½

Rock Creek

Wagons

At dusk July 2, 1863, the Gibraltar Brigade saved the guns on the top of Cemetery Hill at Gettysburg from being captured by the Rebels.

In spite of great victories at Gettysburg and on the Mississippi at Vicksburg, the war was still going on and Lincoln's Army needed more soldiers. A draft had begun, and new "conscripts" were arriving in Yankee camps.

Men in some parts of the country didn't want to be forced to go to the army. In New York City there were riots where people carried signs and violently protested being in the draft. These disturbances were called the Draft Riots. John McClure went with the Gibraltar Brigade to help stop the riots.

Harbor
Governors Island new York
Aug 25th '63

Dear Sister

This morning I thought I would write you a few lines to let you know where I am &c. I am well at present and us boys are enjoying ourselves hugely. We landed on this island two days ago. I supose we came here for the purpose of enforcing the draft in New York. We came here from Alexandria on the Steamer Atlantic. Had a long ride. Some of the boys got verry sick but I did not. We was on board of the ship for four days. Glad enough when we got on the island.

You spoke to me about sending my likeness to you. I will do it the first opportunity. I would have had it taken at Alexandria, but I did not have verry good clothes. I think if we lay around New York verry long we will get fat. I can sit here on the grass in the shade and see New York & Brooklin and Jersy Citty all just across the river from us. There is a lot of Foreigners come in here by the ship loads evry week. One of our boys got hurt on board the ship. He was helping to unload the baggage and fell through the hatch hole of the ship from the hurricane deck to the bottom. I guess he will get well; his name is Fred Yocum. I cant write verry much more this morning. We have not got our tents yet. I will write again soon. Tell Henderson I will write to him tell him he had better come out and see us. I dont think there will be much chance for me to go home but if there is any chance I will come. I have got about $70. laid up for that purpose but you need not look for me until you see me coming.

Old Abe is not giving any furloughs now.

From your Brother,

John R. McClure

After Gettysburg and the Draft Riots, General Meade, the general of Gettysburg, took the Army of the Potomac back to camp. Robert E. Lee had his Southern soldiers nearby. Sometimes one army would come out to see where the other army was and fight a little. But both sides seemed too worn out to do real battle. John McClure's letter shows he now thought war was not fun at all—in fact it was horrible. "If ever Bob (his brother) wants to enlist, I want you to keep him from it," he writes.

Camp across the Rappehannoc, Beverly ford, VA.
November 12 th 63

Dear Sister

I received your kind letter written the 2ond. I was glad to hear from you. It found me in good health. And I hope when these few line reaches you they will find you enjoying the same. I cannot exactly tell you where we are, I know this much we are camped in the woods across the rivver. This army has had great times this fall running around. Sometime Mead will retreat and then Old Lee will retreat. Each one trying to get the upperhand of the other.

I suppose you girls have great times with what boys is left at home. If I were in your place I would not make much noise about them. Perhaps they had not room in their waggons for any more or perhaps old preacher would not let george put any more in the waggon. Sis if you and Tont goes up to Rockville I hope you will catch a beaux. If you go give my respects to cousin Newtons girls. Sis the reason that I wrote that I was coming home was because we were at New York and I thought that we would stay there for awhile but I would not come home now if I could because it would cost some monney and it will only be six mongths and a few days untill our time is out and if I live I think I will come home to stay all summer any how. If ever bob wants to enlist I want you to keep him from it because it is not the thing that is is cracked up to be. There is not so much fun in carrying eight days rations. I dont know that he has any notion, but sometimes boys take fool notions although I can stand it—they cant hurt me—it dont make any difference how hard they march because I never had better health in my life. It is a good thing too because Mead marches men harder on less rations and more wormy crackers than any general we ever had.

I sent some monney home by Sargeant Coleman of our company. I have not heard from it yet. I have no more to write at present. Give my respects to all the folks. Write soon to your brother in Virginia.

John R. McClure

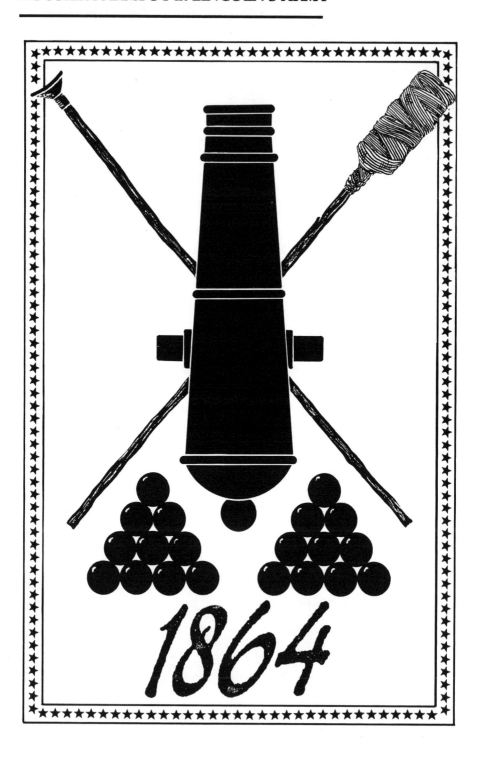

Many battles were being waged in the West. During the winter of 1863-64, the armies waited in the East and tested each other. Sharp exchanges began to occur along the Rapidan river. The Southern Army of Northern Virginia met the Fourteenth's division the first week of February, 1864, in just such an exchange at Morton's Ford on the Rapidan.

Camp near Brandia Station, Va
Feb 8th, 1864

Sister Mary,

I received your letter a few days ago. I was glad to hear from you. I am well and hearty at present. Our division had a fight last saturday. Thank God I came out all right. I dont know how many of our regt lost. We did not have any killed in G Company. Thomas Brity was wounded in the foot. We had to wade the rivver waist deep you had better reckoned it was cold and then had to lay out all night without any fire. You can imagine what a good time we had wadding the Rappidan waist deep and the rebbles shelling us all the time. I supose you had a nice time visiting. I would liked to have been along. I did intend to come home on a fifteen day furlow on the first of January but the order came that no one could go home without he would reenlist. I told them that I could not see it. I guess I can wait until the seventh day of June and then I will take a big furlough.

I have not got the box yet but I supose I will get it within a day or two. My mess mate died the other day (Wm Hill) He was sick two days. Poor fellow he was a good fellow.

I have not got much to write therefore I will bring my letter to a close. Hoping to hear form you soon

From your Brother
John R. McClure

I will frank [send free by special soldier privilege] this letter as I have not stamps.

Robert E. Lee of Virginia.

Camp near Brandia Station, Va.
March 8th, 1864

Sister Mary

I received your letter last night. It found me well and hearty. I had been expecting to hear of Bob enlisting. I dont want him to do it if he does he will be sorry for it. I have told him not to list and if he does it wont be my fault. He will be one of the sickest boys ever you seen before he is out two months.

I wrote a letter to him today and told him what I thought about it. It may all seem to be very nice to be a souldier at home but after he leaves there it wont be so nice. When he gets sworn in he will have to come to the chalk line shure. Out here one regt in our Divission had about 20 such boys come to it as recruits. Old Gen Hays had them drawn up in line and he said that he would like to know what in Hell such boys as them was sent out here for and he had them all sent back home. You had better believe they were the gladdest set of little fellows in world. But it is not often that you will find a General like him.

It surprised me when you told me that Charles Hollingsworth had reenlisted. He wrote to me and said that he could not see the point of going as a vetteran.

I think if I get out of this three years all right I will be doing very well. When I get back home I can lay back on my oars for a while any how. I see that Congress has past an act that men that have served three years will not be drafted. You need not be any ways uneasy about me enlisting I have got enough of it for awhile. I did write to Tom Thompson and told him that I had went in for three more years but I was joking.

Tell Bob if he wants to come to the army so bad to get a job with some officer to take care of his horse or something. Then he can see what souldiering is.

If he is not in to big a hurry, he might come out with Tom Bailey or Boon or some other good Officer and stay awhile.

I have no more to write of importance. Hoping to hear from you soon

From your Brother

John McClure

P.S. Give my best to Aunt Jane and all the rest of the folks.
J. Mc

Finally, U. S. Grant, John McClure's favorite general, was in charge of the Northern Army and was getting ready to break through Lee's army lines once and for all. Grant, a strong-minded and tough fighter, was determined not to stop fighting, not even one day, till he got to Richmond and stopped the war.

But soon John McClure's time would be up. His regiment would be "mustered out." His letters now show he is thinking about home as much as he is the army.

Camp near Brandia Station, Va.
March 22, 1864

Dear Sister

I will not call this a letter I will call it a few lines. You will find a picture in here from your humble servant. It is not a very good one. I answered your last letter I expect you have got it by this time. You will find 50 cts in here to by some stamps to send to me. And also $5.00 that I will make you a pressent of.

No more at pressent. Write soon.

From your Brother

John R. McClure

P.S. I sent your picture home to you not long ago. I knew it would get all broke up. I would like for you to send me your photograph.

John R. McClure

Camp near Brandia Station, Va
April 3 rd

Dear Sister

I received yours of the 26th last evening. It found me well and hearty. We are still in our old camp and likely to stay here some time yet. Two more short mongths and the 14th Ind. time expires.

You spoke about Tom McClure. I don't know any think about how he is doing his business. It may all be false and I would advise you to say nothing either way. Let ever one attend to their own business and us to our own.

I supose Ann has got to be quite a large lady by this time has she not. I am glad to hear that Bob has got out of the notion of soldiering. What position does Henderson hold in his company? I have just come off Sunday morning inspection. We have Church in our Brigade ever Sabbath. I have no more to write at pressent. Hoping to hear from you soon.

From your brother

John McClure

P.S. Give my best wishes to all enquireing Friends.

The Louisiana Tigers, commanded by Rob Wheat, were a colorful group of Southern soldiers who wore "Zouave" uniforms. They were mostly "toughs" from the streets of New Orleans.

Would Ulysses Grant lead the troops into battle before John got out of the army? Would John have to risk death one more time? The answer was Yes!

May 5th and 6th, 1864, General Grant took his whole army into an area near where they had fought a year before at Chancellorsville. It was a second-growth woods full of small clumps of trees and bushes, hard to pass through. The North and the South fought hard, until even the woods caught fire burning some of the wounded men.

Years later, John McClure told his grandson the story of his part in the battle of The Wilderness.

.   .   .

"It wasn't like a battle at all—it was more like Indian warfare. I hid behind a tree and looked out. Across the way, near enough for me to see, was a Rebel aiming at me. I put my hat on a stick I'd picked up and stuck it out from behind the tree—as bait. Then I saw him peep out of the thicket and I shot him. It was the first time I'd ever seen the man I'd killed, and it was an awful feeling. I went to him and rolled him over. He was young, belonged to the Louisiana Tigers, I think, and he gave one groan and died. I had thought I might get his papers out of his wallet and let his folks at home know—but when I saw his face and heard him groan, I hadn't even the heart to do that."

.   .   .

He returned to the protection of the trees. But within that same afternoon John McClure himself had been shot through the shoulder with a Minié ball. He was taken in excruciating pain by ambulance (a springless farm cart) over rutted roads thirty-six hours to the hospital at Alexandria. Actually, he was lucky. Many others of Grant's wounded had been burned alive in the flames that flashed through the underbrush set on fire by the gunfire.

It was two weeks before John's wounds healed enough for him to write. When he spoke of the shoulder wound, he played it down. From the hospital and now in Pennsylvania, he wrote about his experience and then wrote again just before he was mustered out of the army.

Queen Street Hospital
May 18th 1864

Dear Sister

This is the first time that I have had a chance to write to you. I was wounded on the fifth, the first days fight. My wound is not a bad one. I got a slight wound on my right breast and a flesh wound through the arm. My wounds are getting a long fine. I think I will be able to come home with the regt. I cant write much with my arm and you cant expect a verry long letter.

Give the folks my best wishes tell Ann that I have not for got her yet. I have no more to write at pressent. Write soon.

To your Brother

John McClure

John McClure was in a hospital near Philadelphia. Women nurses played an important role in the war.

Chestnut Hill, Phila Pa
June 10th 1864

Dear Sister

I received a letter from you this morning, the only one for a long time. Your letter found me well and hearty. My wounds are healing fast. I expect to start for Indianna next Monday (the 13th). I supose we will be sent to Indianapolis, there we will get our discharge. There is eleven of my regt here, we will all go together.

You spoke of me not writing very long letters. Well at the time I wrote the last letter to you I did not feel very much like writing. Now I am most to fat and lazy to write you a very long one. Philadelphia is about 10 miles from this Hospital. I have been down once since I have been here. It is a very nice place; the folks are very clever. I supose you have seen the list of the killed and wounded of Co G. Thomas Piety is wounded again for the fifth time. He has a pretty bad wound this time. The folks in this part of the country dont put on as much style as they do out our way. By the way you talk you folks has a buggy. I dont supose Unkle Arch ever uses it. Just put it in the carriage house and let it stand there. I wonder if old charly is alive yet. I never thought to ask you. But no time for asking questions now. I think if I keep my heels I will be at home before long. I cannot tell you what day I will be at home. I will tell you more about it when I get to Indianapolis. You need not answer this letter because I will leave here. I will write soon as I get to the state. Tell Henry I have not forgot him yet. Tell him to have his gun in good order by the time time I get home. I believe I am about through writing for this time. I will write as soon as I get to the State.

From your Brother

John R. McClure

On Saturday, June 17, John McClure arrived at Camp Morton in Indianapolis. His wounds were "nearly well" and soon he was going home to Southern Indiana to the farm.

Indianapolis
Sunday June 18th 1864

Dear Sister

    I arrive here yesterday and I thought I would write you a few lines to let you know where I am. I am getting along fine. I dont know exactly what day I will get home. We expect to be mustered out of the service next Monday (20th) but I dont think we will be at home until the last of the week. I am nearly well. I think I will be at home by the last of next week and probly before. You need not answer this it would be of no use. No more at pressent

From your Brother
John R. McClure

John's cousin and friend in the Fourteenth Regiment, Henderson (Bud) Simpson decided to join the army again in another regiment— Indiana's 120th. After John returned home, Bud wrote a letter to John telling of his return to camp near Washington. D.C. after a trip home to get some recruits for his new regiment. He mentions getting drunk and having a "scrape" with a young lady. "Scrape" probably meant keeping her out a little bit later than what her parents wanted. Rules for young men and women seeing each other were very strict during Civil War times.

Camp Stoneman D.C.
February 7th 1865

Cousin John

Here I am once more on the old Potomacs bleak and barren hills "just like we used to be." I am in some what of a hurry this evening but I'll try and give you an out line of our trip. In the first place in going to town that morning I unintentionally took too much whiskey and when I got by a stove in town I got—But myself and recruits got safely off to Indianapolis. Two were rejected. From there I took transportation to Anapolis Md. and started Tuesday evening—Near Knightstown (Ind Central) our car ran off the track but the train stopped before any damage was done beyond mashing some noses. By this we were detained two hours and missed connections at Columbus O. Staid there almost a day—Got on Central Ohio Road and started for Belaire. When we were about 15 miles of that place and while we were going like a streak of lighting the car we were in ran off the track and went jumping along the cross ties some two hundred yards when we upset. The rest of the train ran about three hundred yards past us before they stopped. Considering the tumble we had but little damage was done. One Soldier of the 11th Ind Inf in the seat behind us was killed. Minard Smith had his right arm slightly fractured—It is getting all right

59

now. By this accident we missed connection at Belaire. Next day we crossed to Benwood and got on the B & O R. R. and on our way through I say our stomping ground at North Branch, Pawpaw Tunnel and Martinsburg. Instead of finding our Regt at Anapolis Md., they were near Washington. We dont know where we are going but think when the river opens that we'll go to Arlington. Thus much for our Soldiering.

It has been storming and snowing all day, but as the Captain and I have a good wall tent and stove we are tolerably comfortable.

Has anything leaked out concerning that scrape of mine with that young lady the last night I was at home? I would not have it get out for anything. Not that I care so much for myself but the injury to would be to her should the neighborhood hear of it. John if you think anything of me and have any respect for her whisper nothing of it. Let me know if anything has got out. Write immediately.

Yours truly in haste

Jas. H. Simpson

P.S. Direct to Co. G 120th Reft, Ind Vol Inf
Ist Brigde, 1st Div. 23 rd A.C.

The last battles of the war played themselves out in 1864, after John R. McClure returned home. Kennesaw Mountain, June 27, The Crater, July 30, Siege of Atlanta, August and September. Then in November, 1864, Sherman began his march through Georgia to the sea, to destroy Confederate resistance. Lee's army was gradually being cut off near Richmond. The war was coming to a close.

In one last letter in our book, Henderson Simpson writes of what it will be like for all of the cousins when everyone has returned from the war and peace becomes a wonderful reality. A month before the letter was written, Lee surrendered to Grant at Appomattox Court House in

Virginia on April 9, 1865. John, Mary Jane, Bob and Anna are now living in their own house on the old property next to Henderson's family home.

Camp 120th Ind
Near Charlotte, N.C.
May 19th, 1865

Dear Cousin

I suppose you think (if you ever think of me at all) that I have forgotten you; but allow me to correct such an eroneous opinion (aint that a big word). You see I will drop in on you occasionally, to remind you that I am still "hunk-a-dora" (Shakspear).

The boys are all well—I'm better than common—Have nothing to do now but attend roll calls, dress parades, and eat— anything you can get—But it is getting lonesome out here; and begins to seem like loseing time (you know I always made the minutes count) playing soldier—But I have plenty of work to occupy all my time fixing up Capts accounts, he being back at the hospital. Dont know what to say or think of what is before us—A thousand "grapevines" fill the camp—One says our Regt guards a waggon train through to Kentucky, another that our whole Corps starts for East-Tenn next week—Still another that we'll start back to the coast and take ship for Texas—I guess the surest guess is to guess nothing at all. There's no telling just now what will be done with us.

I hear you and fat Anna have moved up to the "Old place" to keep house for John—I suppose John has fooled Mrs. Grundy this time.

It will seem so much like old times, when I get home, to visit you up there. It seems but yesterday since I used to walk up there— bare legged-pants rolled up—Dont I remember! How glad I'd be when I got to the shady woods beyond Mr. Purcells, and then when I got to the turn on the hill I'd raise a squawk and start off on the double quick. Maybe some of you would come out to the fence to meet me.(You saw me so seldom)—I can see some of you yet, standing on the third or fourth plank, while your toes stuck through the cracks like a row of turtle heads—But those dear old days can never come again—But we thought then some times that we saw awful hard times, awful.

The past is dead—Let the dead bury the dead, while we build castles in the golden tinted clouds of the future. I must smile just a little when I think of the dignified family at the Old place. I see you all to-night—There's John over there in the corner. His boots are off, one foot's up 45 degrees on the jam, the other stuck out at right angles across the hearth. He's smoking, and as he lazily puffs the blue clouds around he stares very hard at you over in the other corner. Now he seems lost in the ceiling—I know what he's thinking of—Thinks he will have Mrs. Some-body over there in the corner some of these days—It's after taps—Annie has become sleepy and says "Sis I cant turn this heel"—You, well may-be you're mending that coat of John's— maybe you're reading The Ledger—It'll seem lonesome to you at first, yet although I am sorry you left us I think it is a good idea—Think I'll keep Bachelor's Hall when I get home up in Mr. Long's cabin. Wouldn't it be Romantic—So "mentisental" after coming in out of the harvest field to go after water—fry a little bacon—&c &c &c &c &c &c.

Tell John I am looking for that letter from him. Awful lonesome out here. Don't get letters from any one but Ma & Henry.

Write and tell me all the news—and I'll promise to answer you when the fit comes on. If this letter helps you to pass off as pleasantly as much time as it has me it has filled "its mission."

I remain very respectfully your

Most dutifull Cousin

Jas H. Simpson

AFTERWORD

John did marry his girlfriend, Fanny; Henderson Simpson married also, and many of the boys' dreams of peaceful farming came to pass.

But the lives of John McClure and Henderson would never be the same. They talked of the war at family gatherings, went to regimental reunions, and John finally "heard taps played for the last time," as reported by the newspapers in 1922. We can remember John, and all the soldiers he represents, for their courage, tenacity, humor and honesty. Both sides, North and South fought bravely for what they believed in, and when they were done, the slaves were free and the United States was one Union again. This is a proud heritage to pass on to any coming generation.

Frances "Fanny" Purcell was John McClure's "girl I left behind me."

John McClure came home from the Civil War, married "Fanny" and became a farmer.

Friendship and loyalty for soldiers of both North and South didn't end with the war. John R. McClure (top row, second from right) is shown at a regimental reunion at the turn of the century.

Mary Jane McClure, John's sister, wrote to John and received many letters during the war.

John McClure, his wife, children and dog on the family farm about 1890.

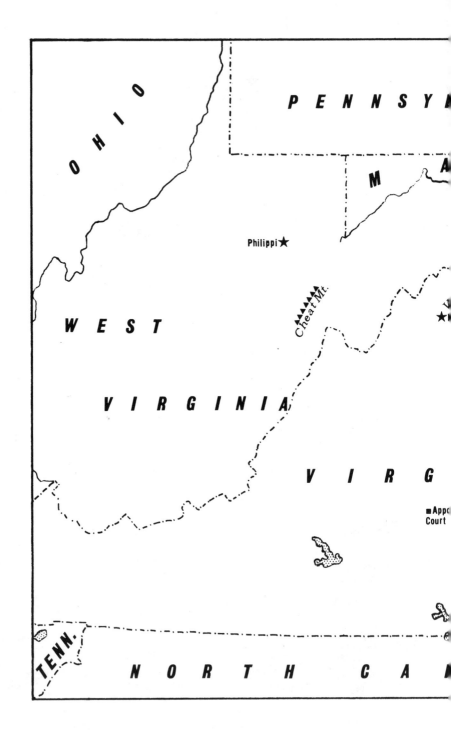

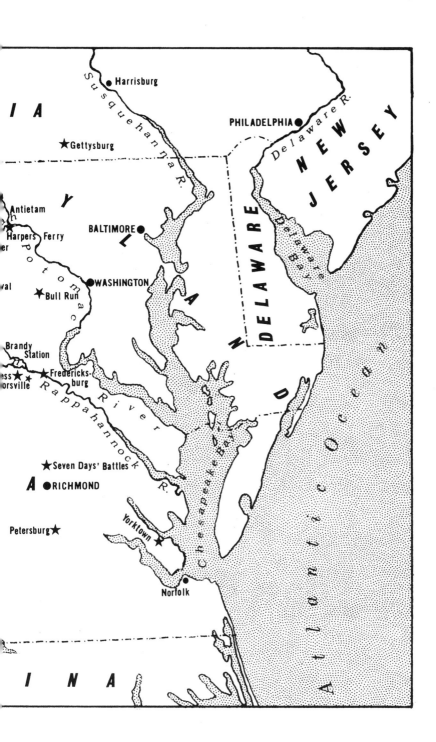

I A

Susquehanna R.

● Harrisburg

★ Gettysburg

PHILADELPHIA ●

Delaware R.

NEW JERSEY

Y

Antietam

Harpers Ferry

BALTIMORE ●

DELAWARE

L

Delaware Bay

A

Potomac

● WASHINGTON

★ Bull Run

N

D

val

Brandy Station

ss ★
orsville ★

★ Fredericks-burg

Rappahannock River

River

Chesapeake Bay

Atlantic Ocean

★ Seven Days' Battles

A ● RICHMOND

Petersburg ★

Yorktown ★

Norfolk ●

I N A